Police Officer

Written by Sue Barraclough
Photography by Chris Fairclough

W

FRANKLIN WATTS

LONDON • SYDNEY

First published in 2005 by Franklin Watts
96 Leonard Street, London EC2A 4XD

Franklin Watts Australia
45-51 Huntley Street, Alexandria, NSW 2015

© Franklin Watts 2005

Editors: Caryn Jenner, Sarah Ridley
Designer: Jemima Lumley
Art direction: Jonathan Hair
Photography: Chris Fairclough

The publisher wishes to thank: Lorraine and Embassy, Debbie and
Farleigh, Michelle and Coxie, Steve, Dick, Andy and Noel of the
London Metropolitan Police Service; Sammah and Sulaymah;
Emma Shaw and St John's School, Fulham, London for their
assistance with the book.

A CIP catalogue record for this book
is available from the British Library

ISBN 0 7496 6054 6

Dewey decimal classification number: 363.2'2

Printed in China

Contents

I am a police officer

POLICE
HORSE PATROL
STATION

My name is
Lorraine and
I work at a
mounted police
unit in London.

This means that instead of driving a police car, I ride a police horse. My horse is called Embassy.

On patrol

A normal working day includes
a four hour patrol around the
streets. My horse is trained to be
calm in traffic.

We always go out on patrol with another officer. We are high up on the horses so we can see what is going on around us.

Making an arrest

A mounted police officer can be useful in making an arrest. A police car can't follow a suspect into a park, but we can.

I use my radio
to call the station
for more police
officers.

A police car is sent
from the station to
collect the suspect.

Talking about my job

When I go on patrol I talk to the people that I meet so that they know I am there to help.

Sometimes I go into schools to talk to
the children about my job.

Looking after Embassy

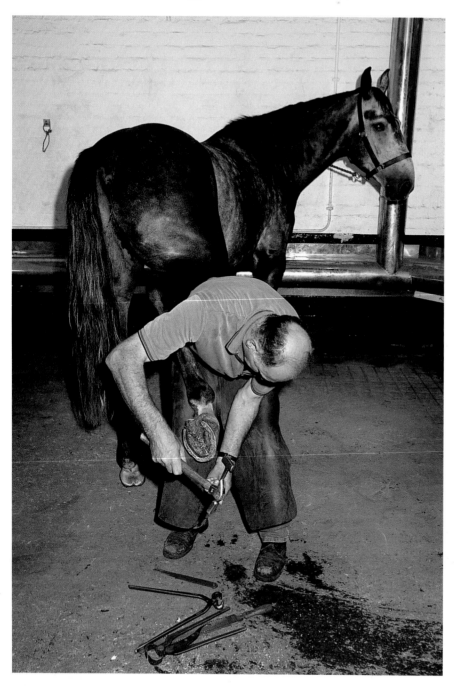

Most of our police work involves walking along city streets. Our farrier puts new metal shoes on Embassy's feet every month to protect them.

Each police
horse has its
own stable, to
rest and sleep
in. I keep
Embassy's stable
clean and tidy.

Special duties

Before we go to a special event,
we have a meeting. We are told
where we are going and what
our duties will be.

Once I have put
on the right
uniform and
equipment, we
are ready to set
off. To work at
a football match,
I wear special
protective gear.
Embassy has
special gear too.

Working at a football match

Many police officers work at a football match, on foot and on horseback. Our bright yellow jackets mean that we can be seen clearly.

We work with other police
officers to make sure that the
huge crowds of football fans get
out of the football ground safely.

Controlling a crowd

From horseback, I can see over the top of the crowd and spot problems. I use my megaphone to shout instructions.

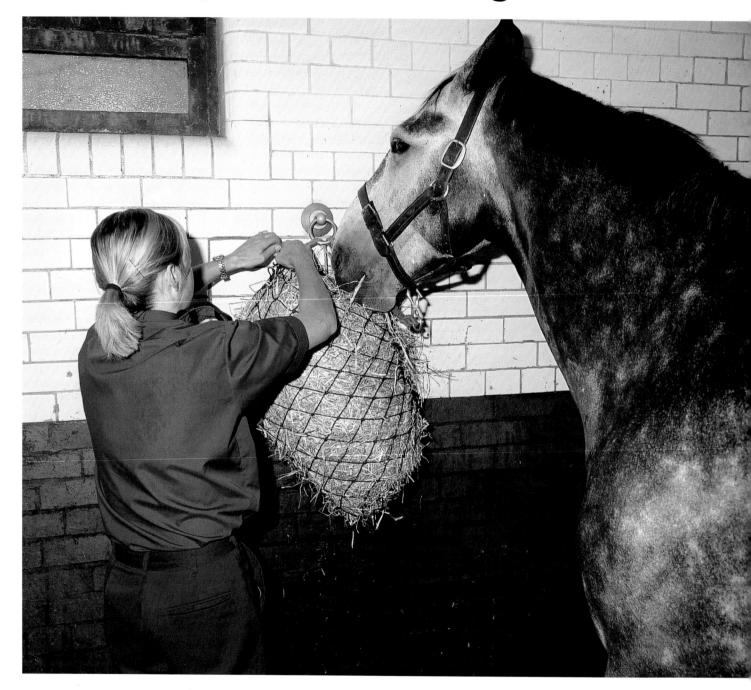

When we arrive back from patrol, I groom and feed Embassy. The equipment is cleaned and put away.

Writing reports and paperwork

I use a computer to
do my paperwork.
I write a report on
what has happened
during the day.
Then it's time to
go home.

Mounted police equipment

This police **helmet** is worn for everyday patrols.

Handcuffs are sometimes used when a police officer makes an arrest.

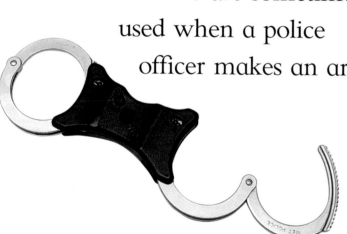

Riding boots have metal spurs on the heels that are used to control the horse.

A **radio** is clipped to the uniform so that an officer can keep in touch with the police station.

This **helmet** is specially designed to protect the head and face. It forms part of the protective gear we wear to special events.

A **megaphone** helps a police officer to shout instructions clearly by making the voice louder.

The mounted police

Embassy is eight years old and has been a police horse for two years. He had about six months training when he first arrived to make sure he was calm in rowdy crowds or busy traffic.

51
EMBASSY

Once trained, he was given a nameplate with his own number. Embassy goes on regular training courses for special events.

Officers get to know and love their horses but they are not pets, they are working animals.

To become a mounted police officer, you need to have been in the police service for two years. Previous work with horses is not essential because training includes learning how to look after horses and their health, and also how to ride.

Glossary and index